ACCORDION FAVORITES

Arranged by GARY MEISNER

CONTENTS

HAL•LEONARD® CORPORATION

7777 W. BLUEMOUND RD. P.O. BOX 13819 MILWAUKEE, WI 53213

Cabaret
(From the Musical "CABARET")

Music by John Kander
Words by Fred Ebb

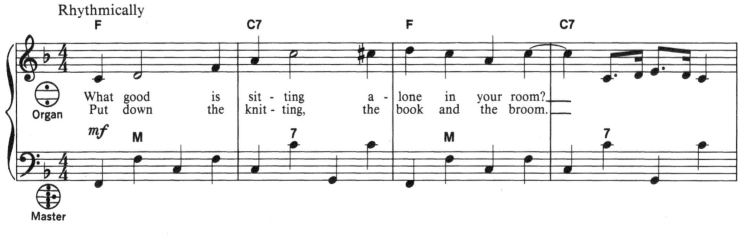

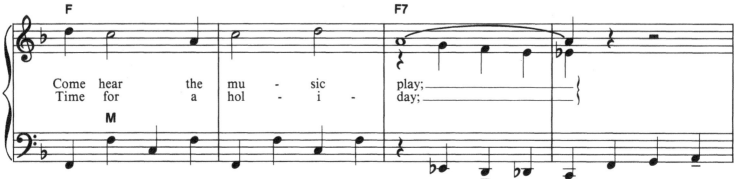

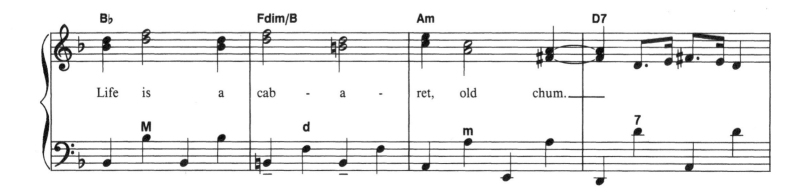

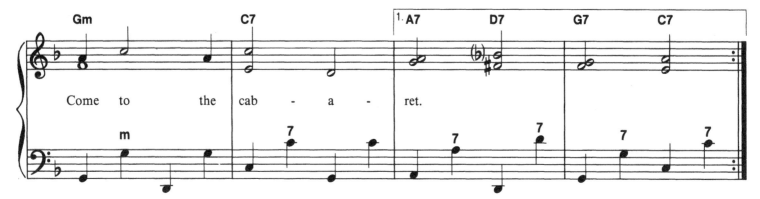

ret. _____ Come taste the wine, Come hear the

band, Come blow the horn, start cel - e - bra - ting,

Right this way, your ta - ble's wait - ing. No use per - mit - ting some

pro - phet of doom _____ to wipe ev - 'ry smile a -

4

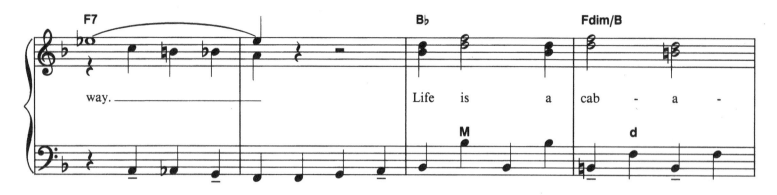

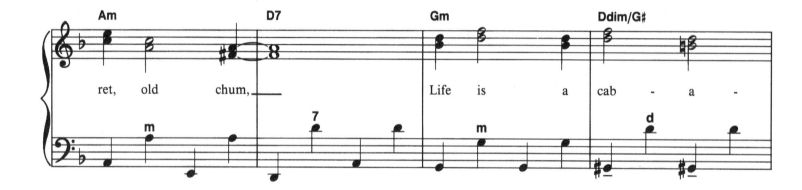

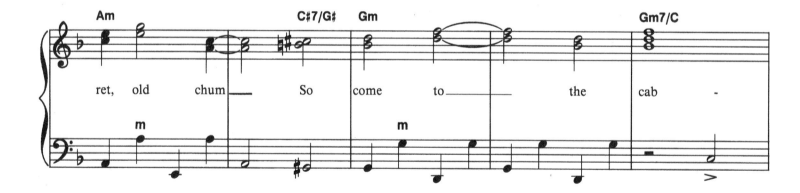

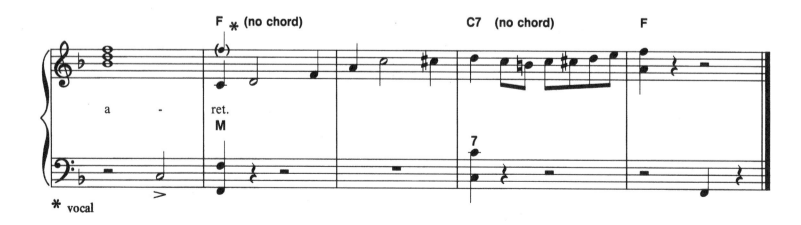

* vocal

Memory

(From "CATS")

Text by Trevor Nunn after T.S. Eliot
Music by Andrew Lloyd Webber

6

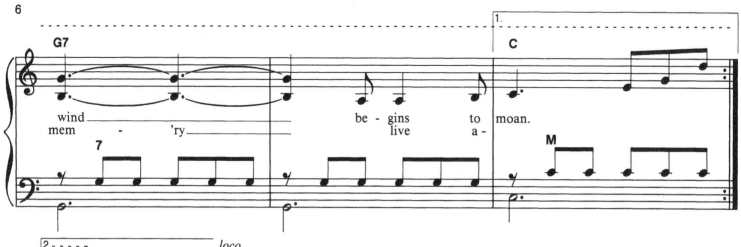

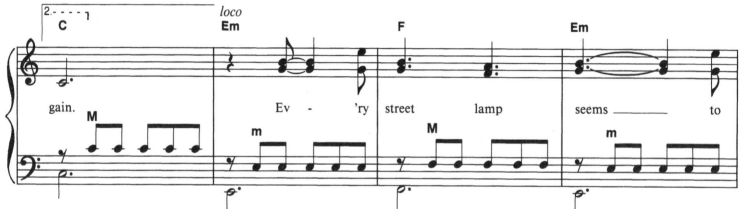

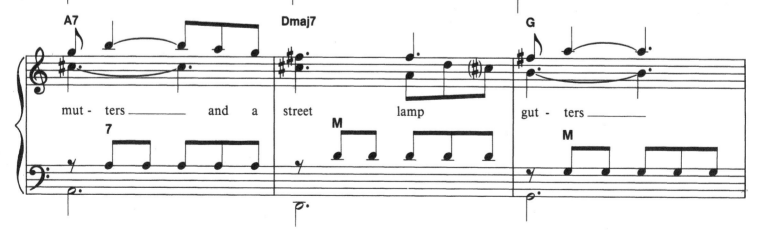

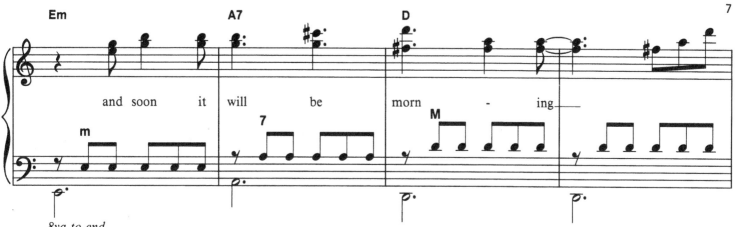

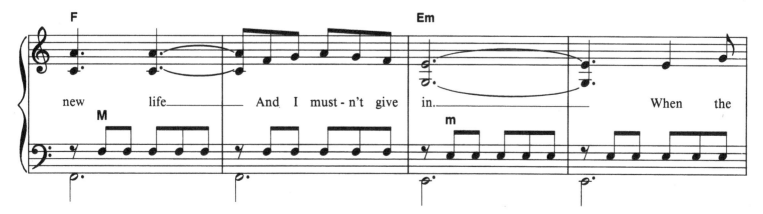

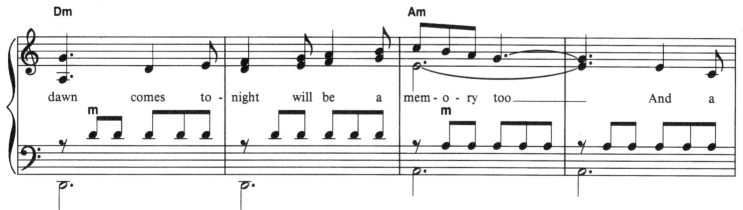

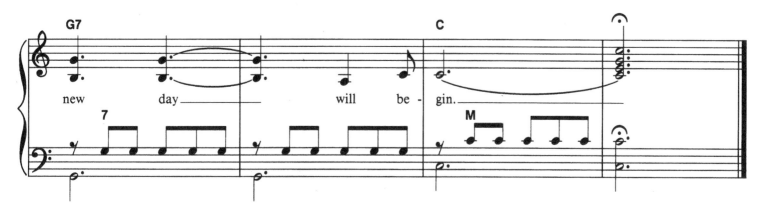

Can't Help Falling In Love

Words and Music by George Weiss,
Hugo Peretti, and Luigi Creatore

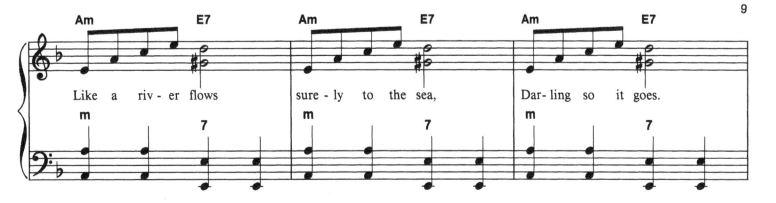

Like a riv-er flows sure-ly to the sea, Dar-ling so it goes.

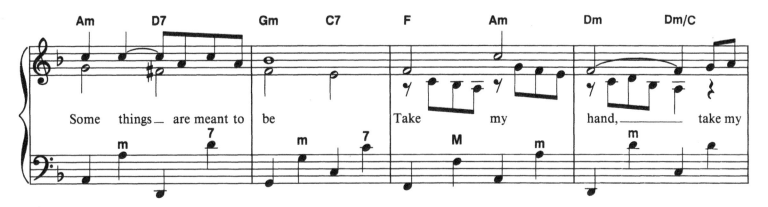

Some things__ are meant to be Take my hand,_____ take my

whole life too._____ For I can't help fall-ing in

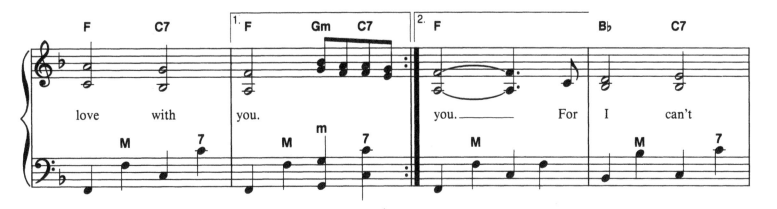

love with you. you._____ For I can't

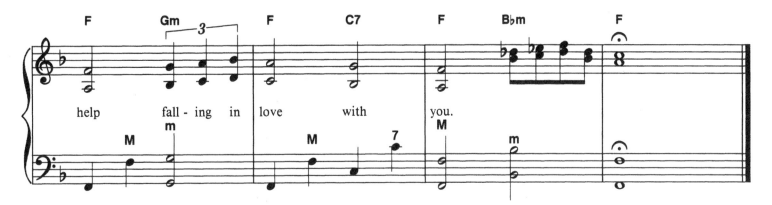

help fall-ing in love with you.

Can't Smile Without You

Words and Music by Chris Arnold,
David Martin and Geoff Morrow

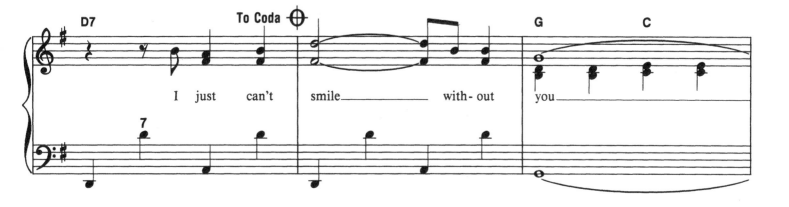

bright-ened my day. Who'd-a be-lieved that you were part of a dream.

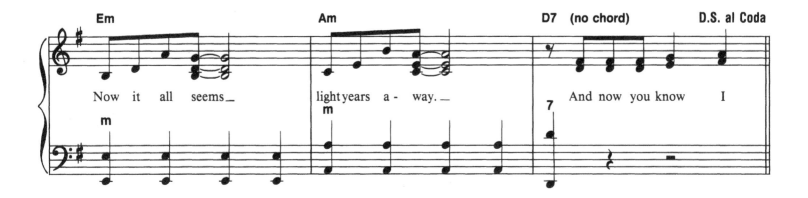

Now it all seems light years a-way. And now you know I

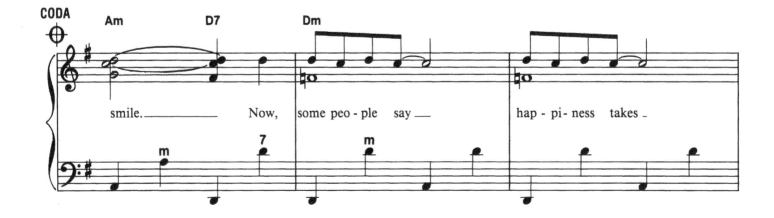

smile. Now, some peo-ple say hap-pi-ness takes

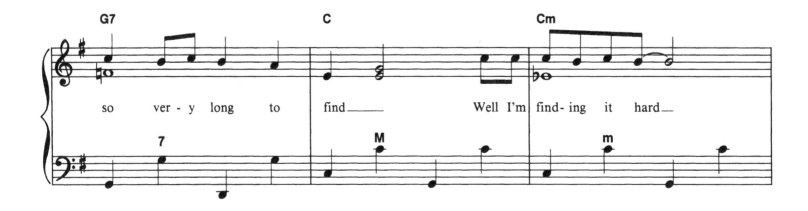

so ver-y long to find Well I'm find-ing it hard

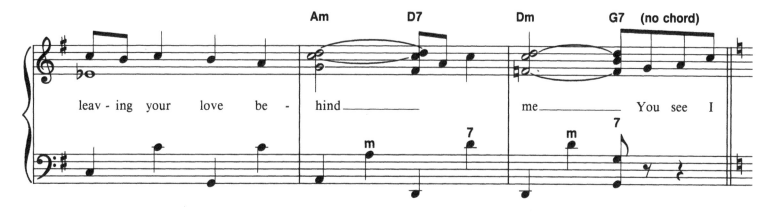

leav - ing your love be - hind _____ me _____ You see I

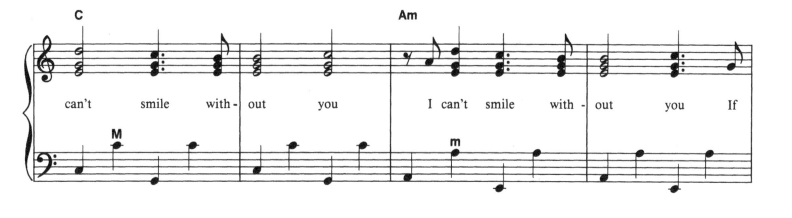

can't smile with - out you I can't smile with - out you If

you ____ on - ly knew what I'm ____ go - ing through I just can't

smile with- out you. _____

Could I Have This Dance

Words and Music by
Wayland Holyfield and Bob House

Slow Country Waltz

I'll al-ways re-mem-ber the song they were play-ing the
al-ways re-mem-ber that mag-ic mo-ment, when

first time we danced and I knew. As we swayed to the
I held you close to me. As we moved to-

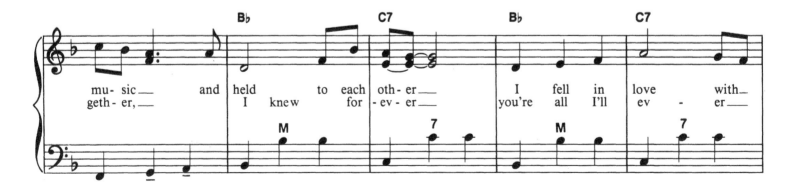

mu-sic and held to each oth-er I fell in love with
geth-er, I knew for-ev-er you're all I'll ev - er

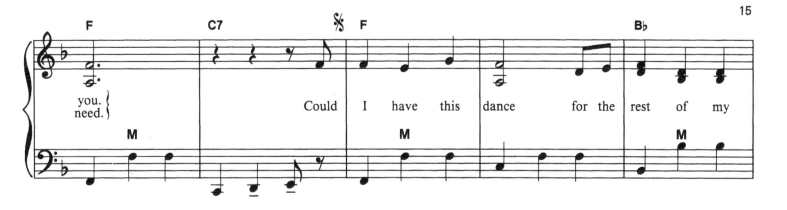

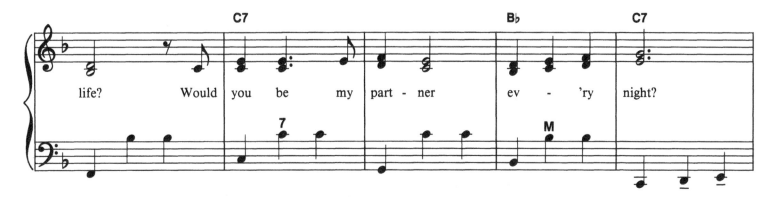

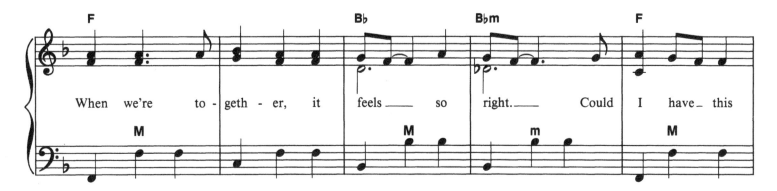

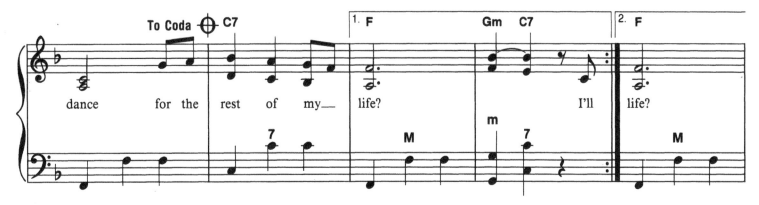

Don't Cry Out Loud

Words and Music by
Carole Bayer Sager and Peter Allen

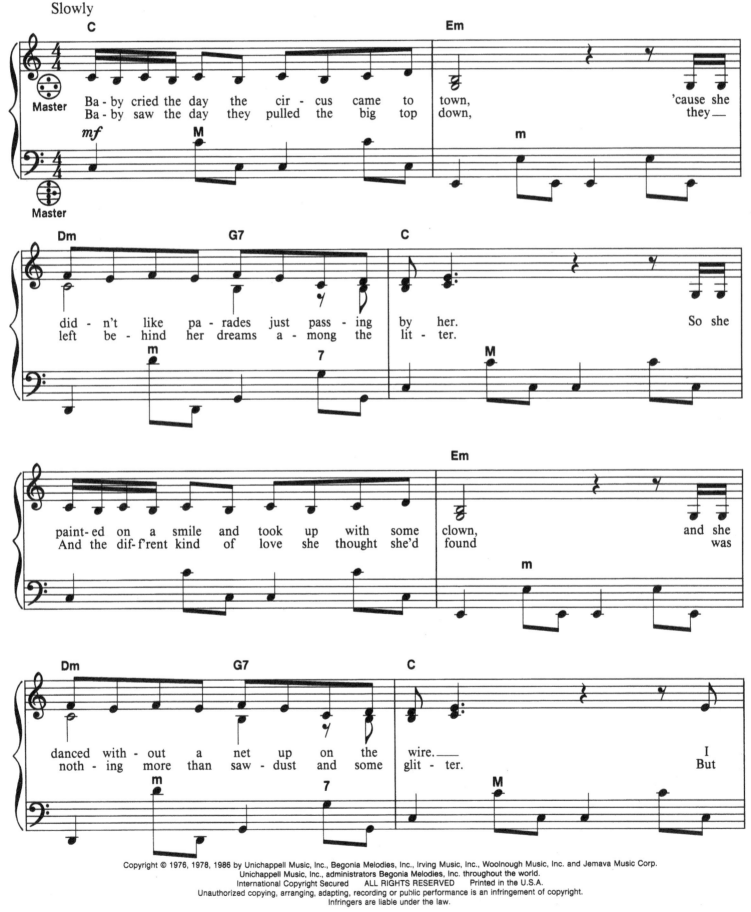

Edelweiss
(From "THE SOUND OF MUSIC")

Words by Oscar Hammerstein II
Music by Richard Rodgers

Slowly with expression

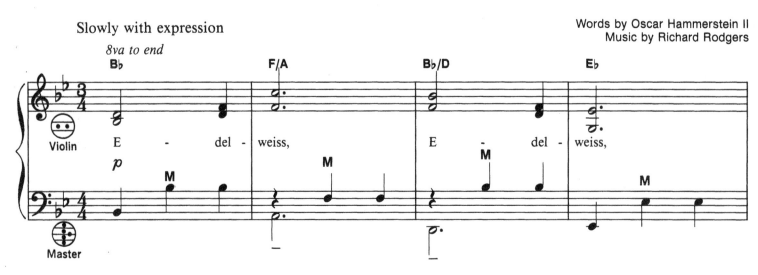

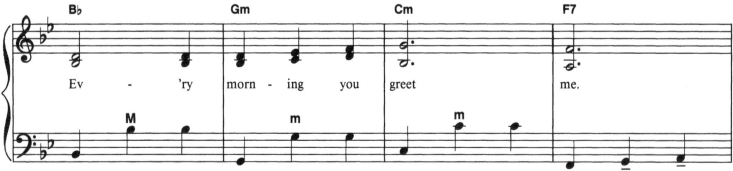

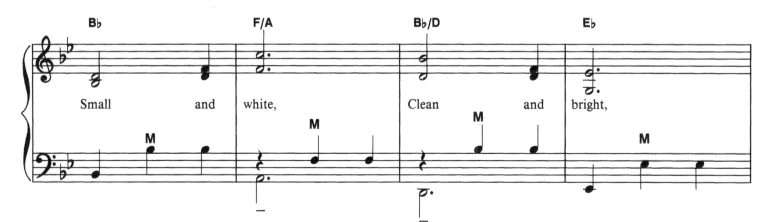

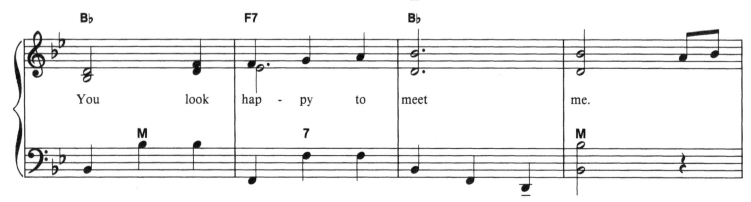

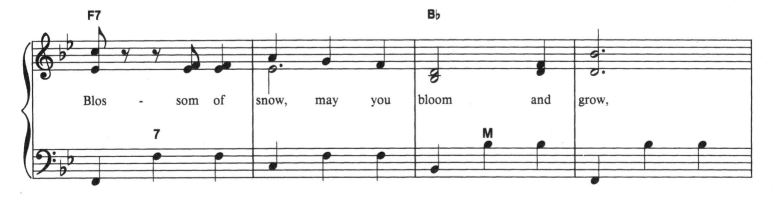

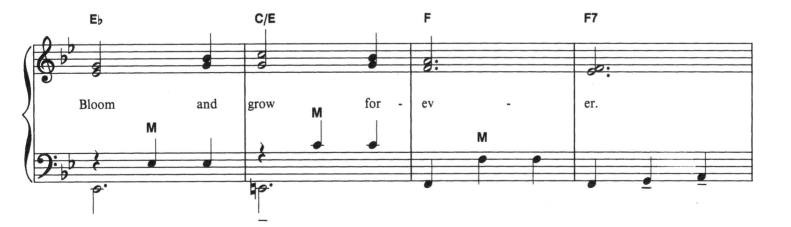

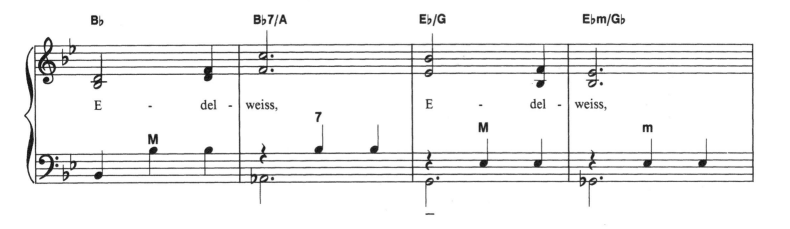

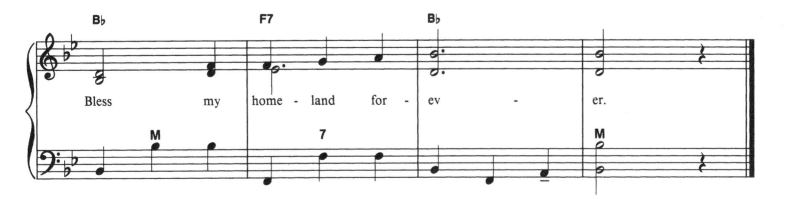

Endless Love

Words and Music by
Lionel Richie

step I make
sist your charms
And
And I love

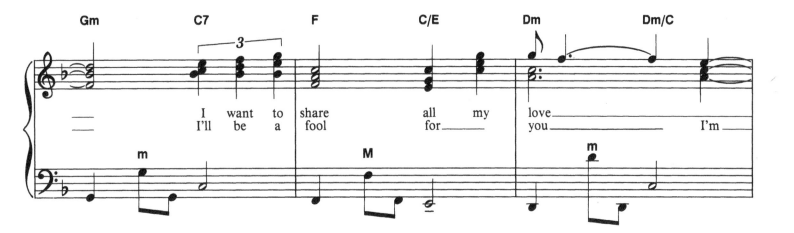

I want to share all my love
I'll be a fool for you I'm

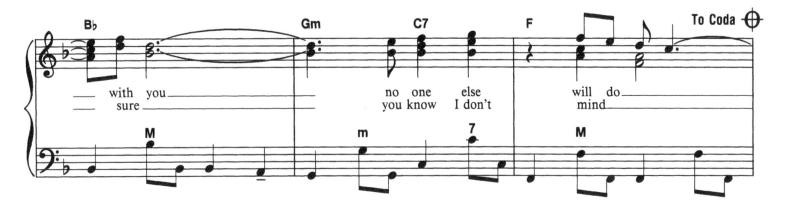

with you no one else will do
sure you know I don't mind

To Coda ⊕

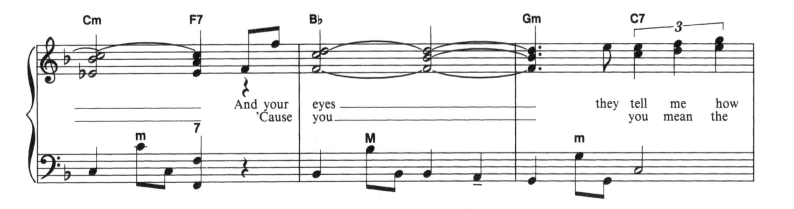

And your eyes they tell me how
'Cause you you mean the

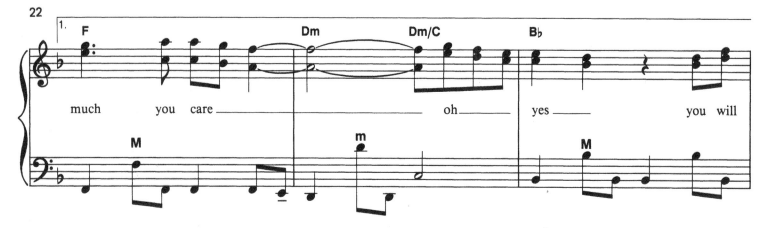

much you care _____ oh _____ yes _____ you will

al - ways be My end - less

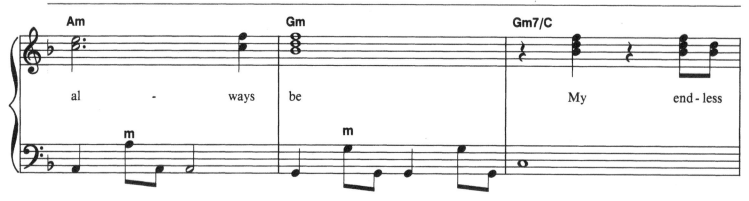

love. world to me _____

_____ Oh I know I found _____ in

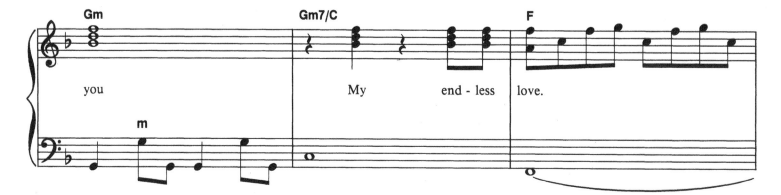

you My end - less love.

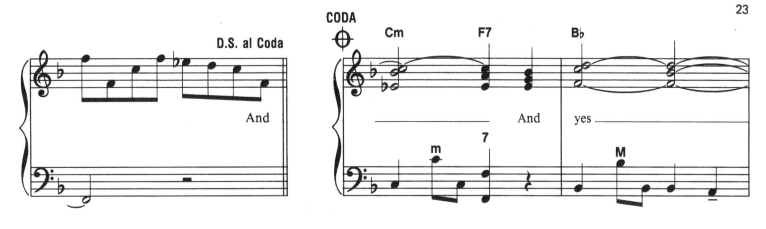

D.S. al Coda

And

CODA

Cm F7 Bb

And yes

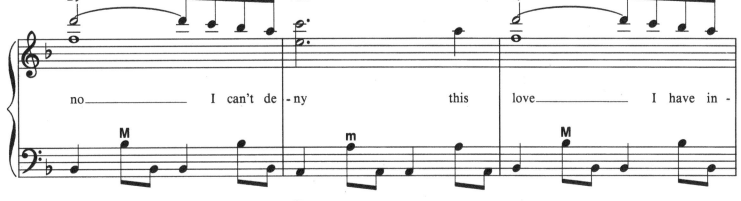

Gm C7 F Dm

You'll be the on - ly one Oh

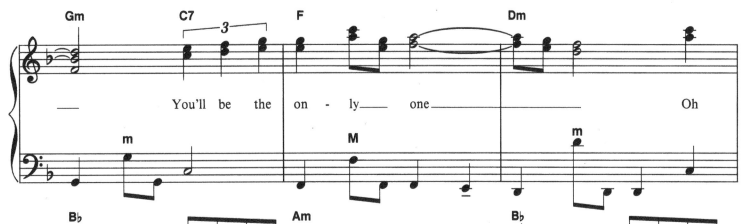

Bb Am Bb

no I can't de - ny this love I have in -

Am Bb Am

side And I'll give it all to you my

Gm Gm7/C F

love My end - less love
rit.

Green Green Grass Of Home

Words and Music by
Curly Putman

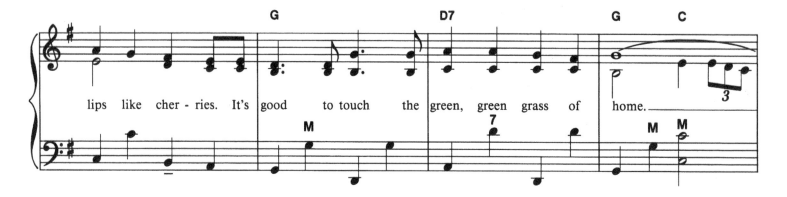

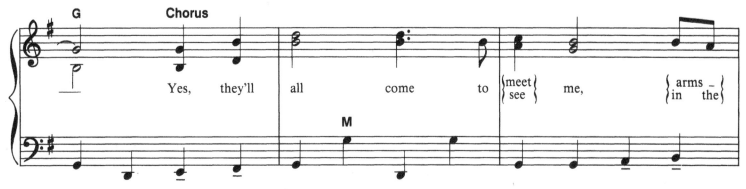

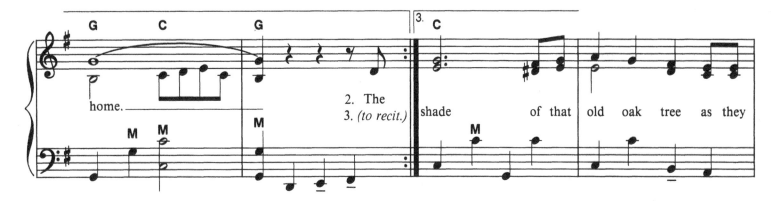

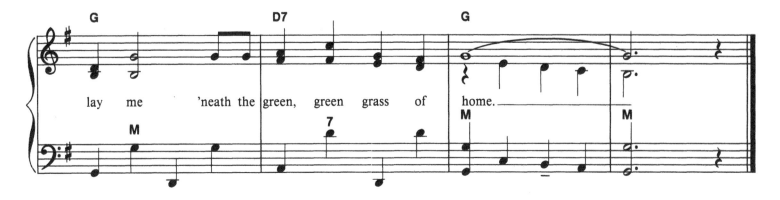

Additional Lyrics

(Recitation)

Then I awake and look around me
At four gray walls that surround me
And I realize that I was only dreaming.
For there's a guard and there's a sad old padre,
Arm in arm we'll walk at daybreak.
Again I'll touch the green, green grass of home.

Chorus

King Of The Road

Words and Music by
Roger Miller

With a bounce

1,3 Trail- er___ for sale___ or rent, rooms___ to let
2 Third box- car mid - night train,___ des - ti - na- tion:

fif - ty cents.___ No phone,___ no pool,___ no pets;___
Ban- gor, Maine.___ Old worn - out suit___ and shoes;___

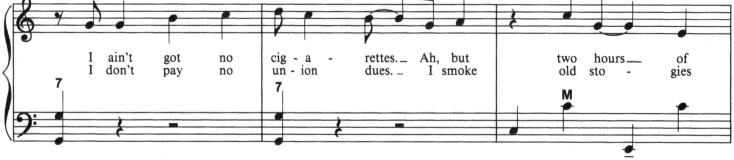

I ain't got no cig - a - rettes.___ Ah, but two hours___ of
I don't pay no un - ion dues. I smoke old sto - gies

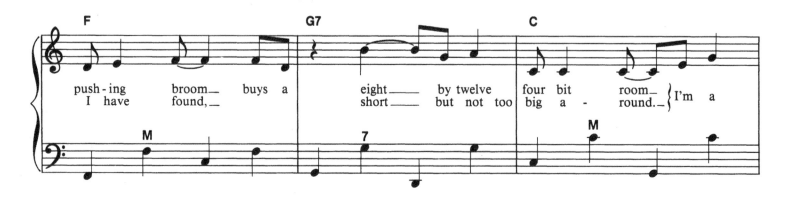

push - ing broom___ buys a eight___ by twelve four bit room.___ {I'm a
I have found,___ short___ but not too big a - round.___

27

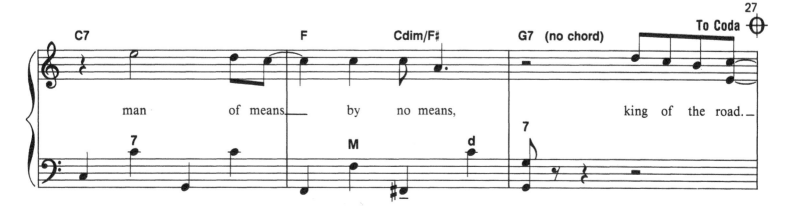

Love Me Tender

Words and Music by
Elvis Presley and Vera Matson

Love me ten - der, love me sweet;
Love me ten - der love me long;
(See additional lyrics)

Nev - er let me
Take me to your

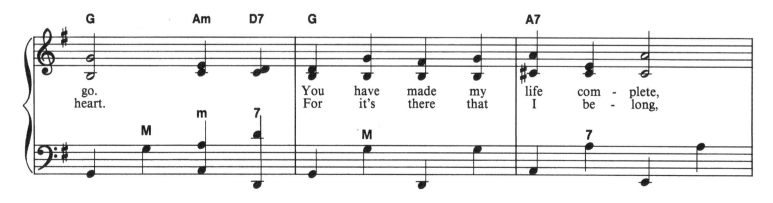

go.
heart.

You have made my life com - plete,
For it's there that I be - long,

Chorus

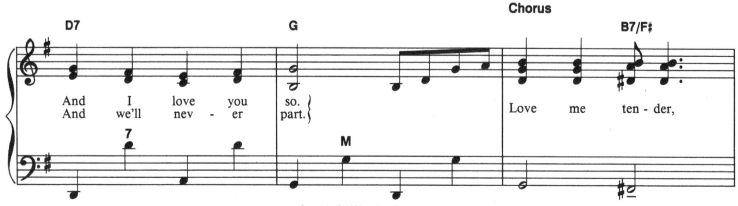

And I love you so.
And we'll nev - er part.

Love me ten - der,

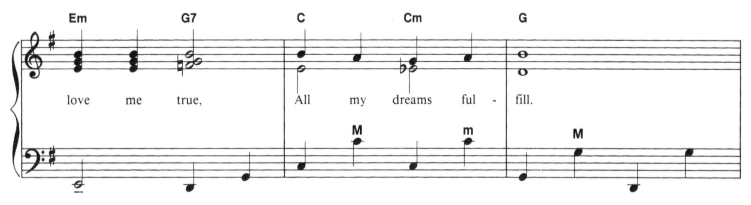

love me true, All my dreams ful - fill.

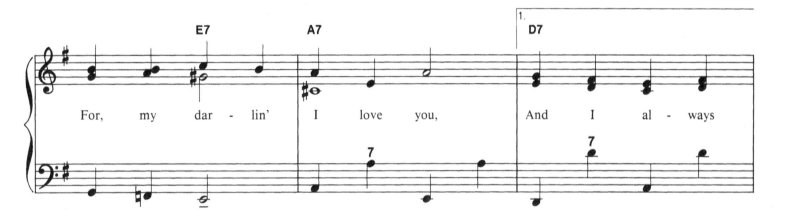

For, my dar - lin' I love you, And I al - ways

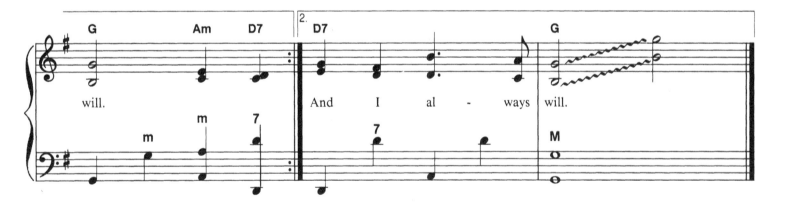

will. And I al - ways will.

Additional Lyrics

3. Love me tender, love me dear;
   Tell me you are mine.
   I'll be yours through all the years,
   Till the end of time.
   Chorus

4. When at last my dreams come true,
   Darling, this I know:
   Happiness will follow you
   Everywhere you go.
   Chorus

More

(Theme From MONDO CANE)

English Words by Norman Newell
Music by Riz Ortolani and Nino Oliviero

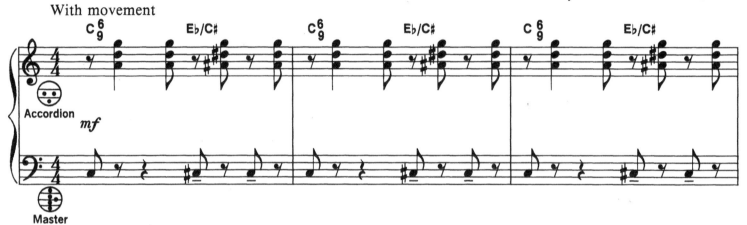

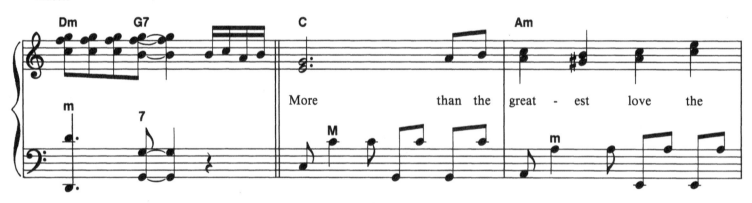

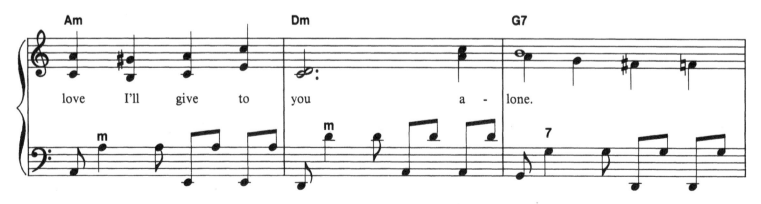

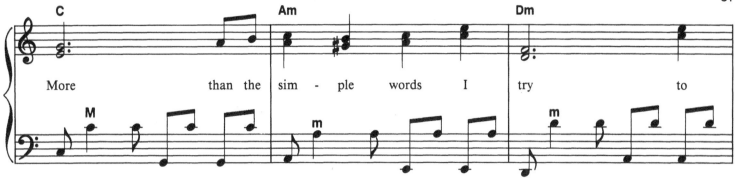

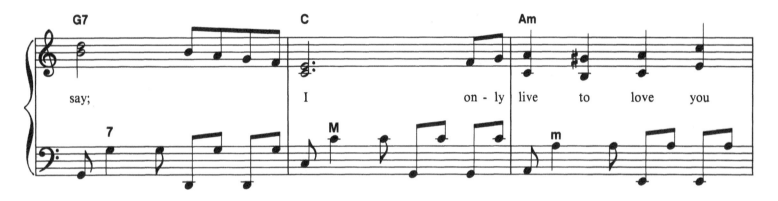

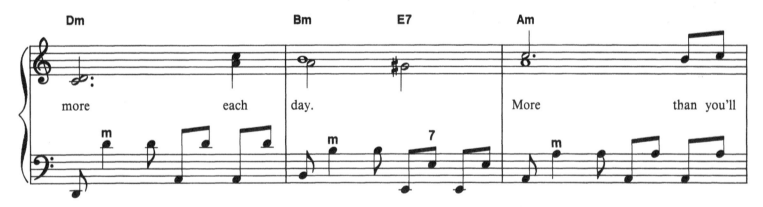

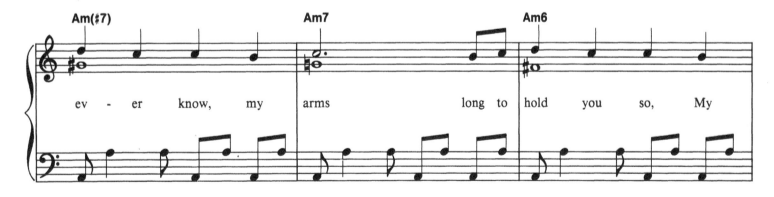

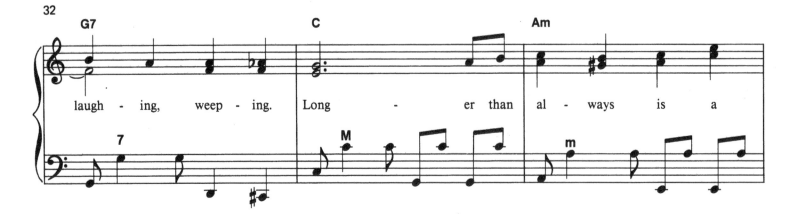

laugh - ing, weep - ing. Long - er than al - ways is a

long long time, But far be -

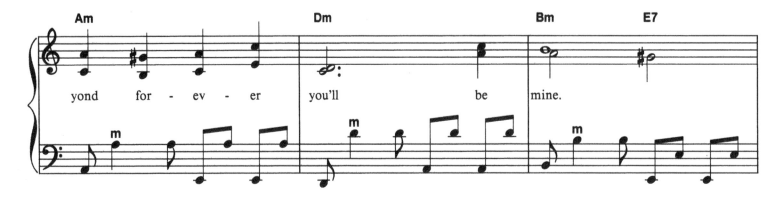

yond for - ev - er you'll be mine.

I know I nev - er lived be - fore and my heart is ver - y

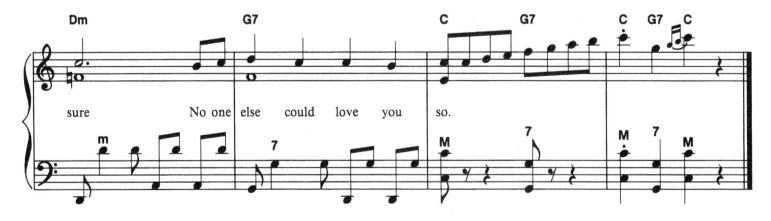

sure No one else could love you so.

People

Words by Bob Merrill
Music by Jule Styne

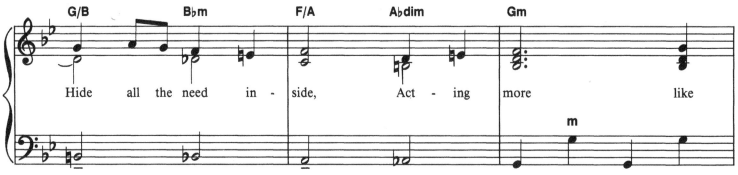

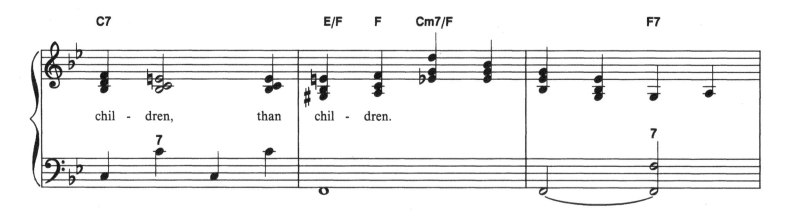

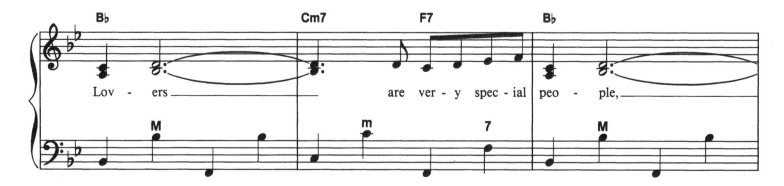

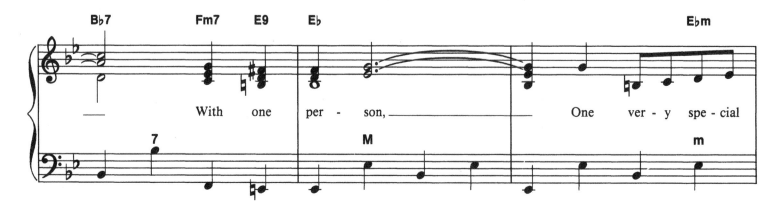

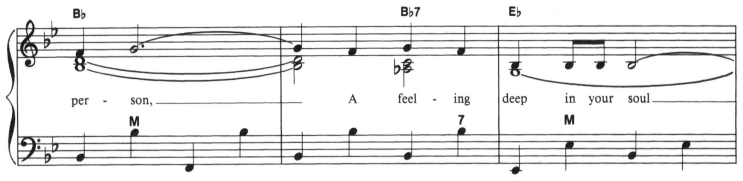

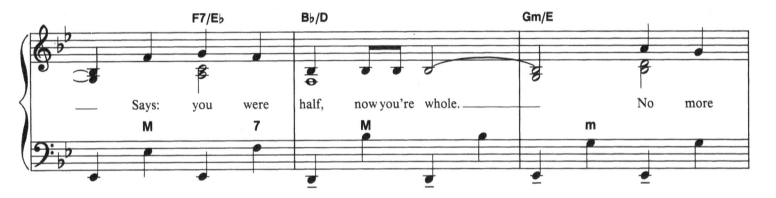

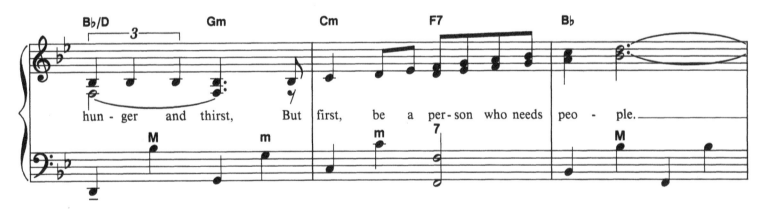

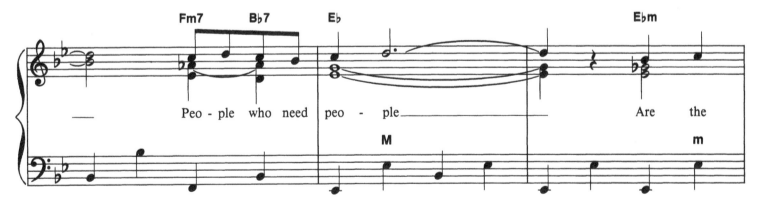

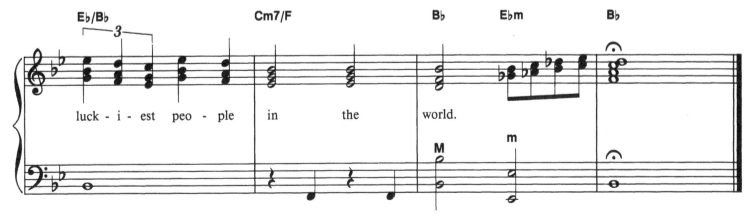

Smoky Mountain Rain

Words and Music by
Kye Fleming and Dennis Morgan

filled my eyes — when I found out she was gone. —

Chorus

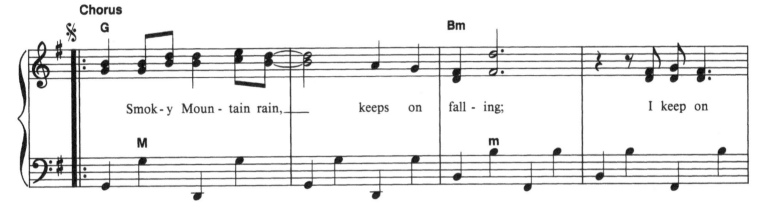

Smok-y Moun-tain rain, — keeps on fall-ing; I keep on

call-ing — her name. — *repeat 3rd time only*

Smok-y Moun-tain rain, — I'll keep on search-ing; I can't go on hurt-ing —

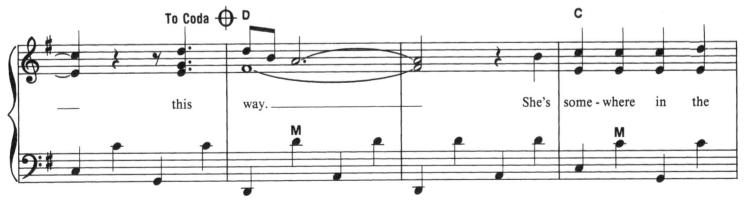

this way. — She's some-where in the

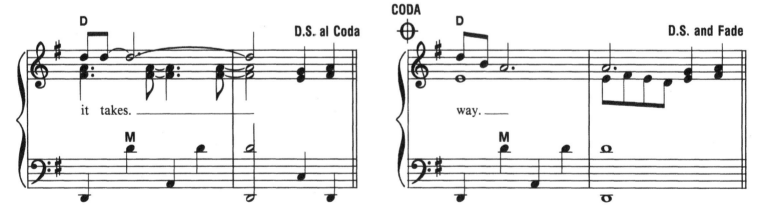

Additional Lyrics

2. I waved a diesel down outside a cafe;
He said that he was going as far as Gatlinburg.
I climbed up in the cab, all wet, and cold, and lonely;
I wiped my eyes and told him about her.
I've got to find her, can you make these big wheels burn?
(To Chorus:)

Song Sung Blue

Words and Music by
Neil Diamond

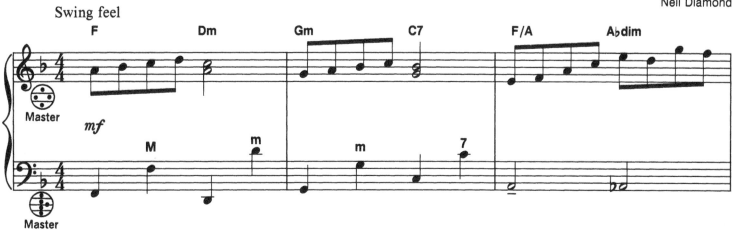

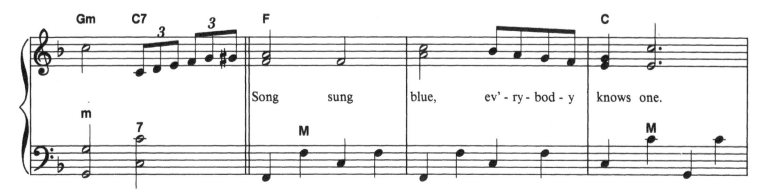

Song sung blue, ev'-ry-bod-y knows one.

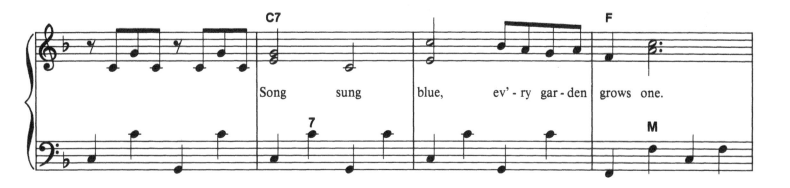

Song sung blue, ev'-ry gar-den grows one.

Me and you___ are sub-ject to___ the

blues now and then.

But when you take the blues, — and make a song,

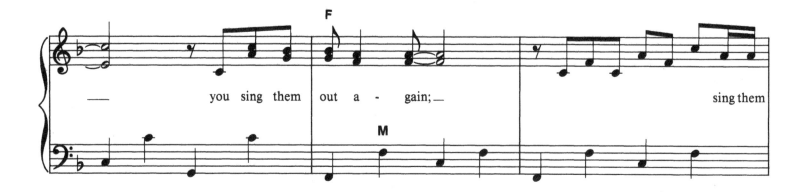

you sing them out a - gain; —

sing them

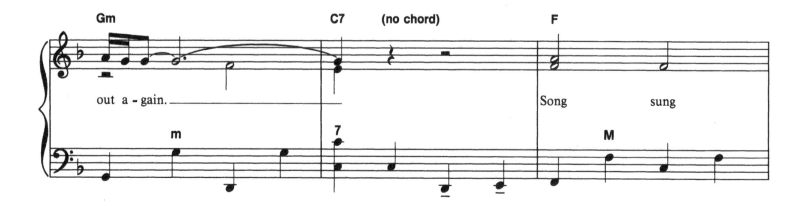

out a - gain. —

Song sung

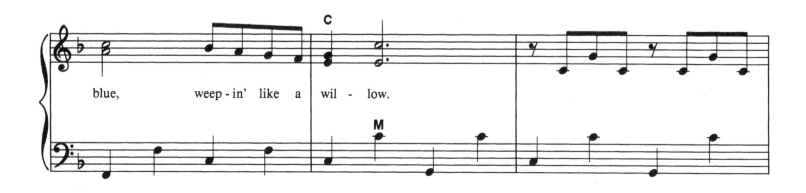

blue, weep - in' like a wil - low.

Song sung blue, sleep-in' on my pil - low.

Fun- ny thing,___ but you can sing___ it with a

cry in your voice___ and, be-fore you know it, start to feel-in' good.___

You sim-ply got no choice.___

Sunrise, Sunset

(From the Musical "FIDDLER ON THE ROOF")

Words by Sheldon Harnick
Music by Jerry Bock

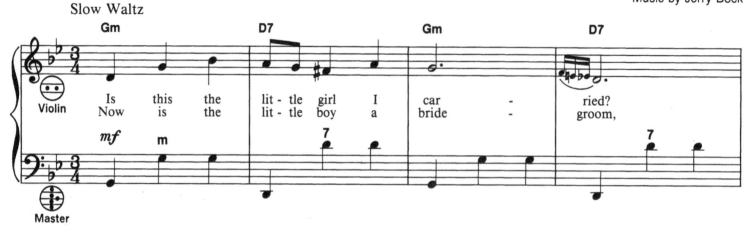

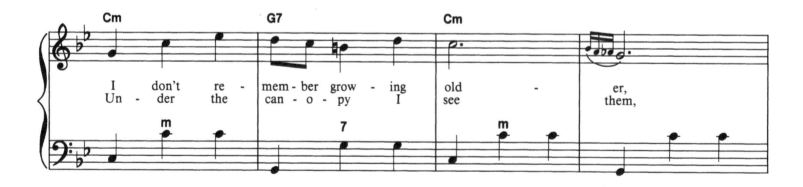

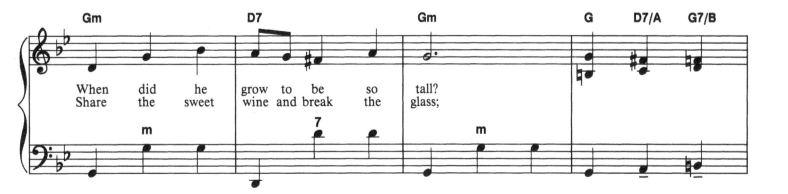

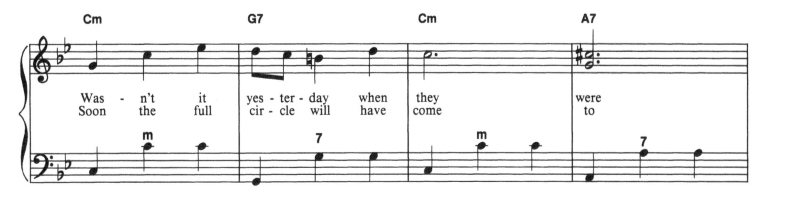

44

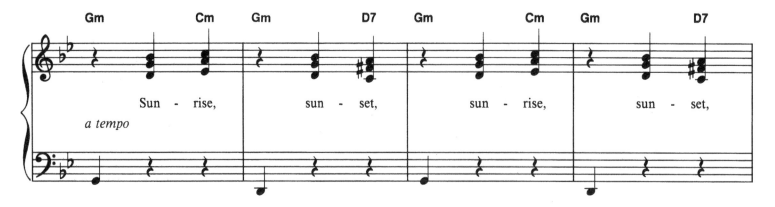

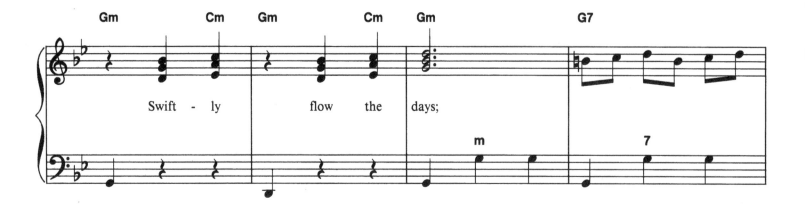

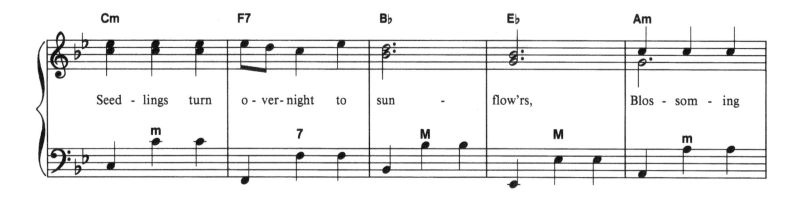

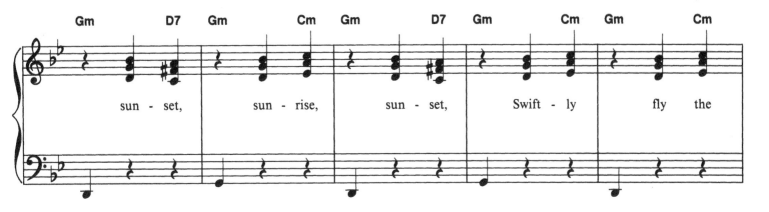

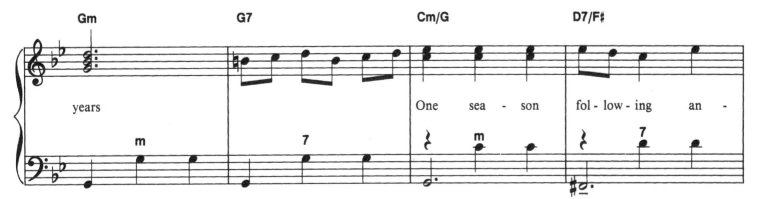

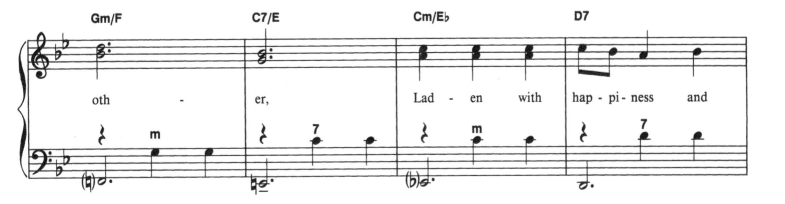

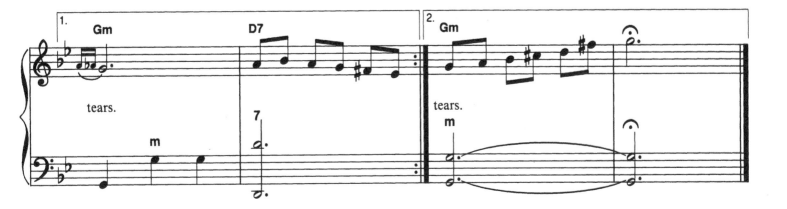

You Needed Me

Words and Music by
Randy Goodrum

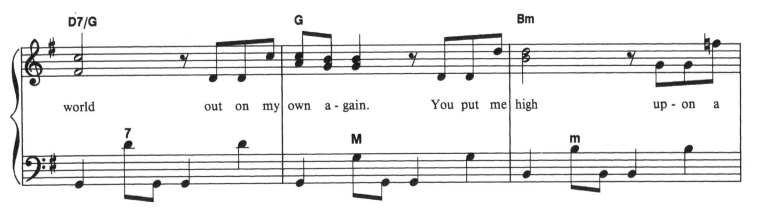

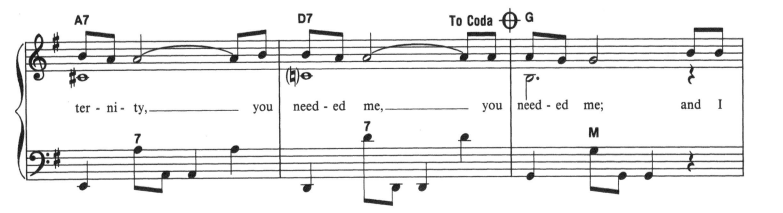

need-ed you___ and you were there___ and I'll nev-er leave. Why should I leave. I'd

be a fool___ 'cause I've fin-'lly found some-one who real-ly cares.

You held my

need-ed me. You need-ed me,___ you

need-ed me.